LEGENDARY LESSONS

DAYS OF THE WEEK TO SEEK

Copyright © 2019 by Kristen Mann ISBN 978-0578-50491-9 All rights reserved. No part of this publication may be reproduced, distributed, or transmitted in any form or by any means, including photocopying, recording, or other electronic or mechanical methods, without the prior written permission of the publisher, except in the case of brief quotations embodied in critical reviews and certain other noncommercial uses permitted by copyright law. For permission requests, write to the publisher, addressed "Attention: Permissions Coordinator," at the email address below.

Kristennicolemann@gmail.com

Ordering Information: Quantity sales. Special discounts are available on quantity purchases by corporations, associations, and others. For details, contact the publisher at the email address above. Orders by U.S. trade bookstores and wholesalers. Please contact Kristen Mann: Kristennicolemann@gmail.com or visit www.growbloomproject.com. Printed in the United States of America.

I'm Legend and welcome to my world. Come on! Let's seek the days of the week together!

Sunday

My mommy wakes me
up for church on Sunday's.
I am most excited about going
to Little Life learning
with all my friends.

Monday

I woke up early in the morning
and I noticed my legs were longer.
Do you notice
when you are growing taller?
I do because I can reach the
treats on the counter
that Daddy and Mommy buys for me.

Tuesday

Pizza is one my favorite foods to eat!
I was so excited to have Pizza for lunch at my Daycare.

Wednesday

Before going to Daycare
I peeked outside and seen
that trees were blowing in the wind.
Daddy made sure
I was dressed in layers to stay warm.

Thursday

When I got home from Daycare
the Cookie Jar lid was
on the kitchen floor.
I hurried to tell Mommy
so we could wash the lid together.
I love washing
dishes with Mommy!

Friday

When Daddy gets
home from working,
he always tickles me and
makes me laugh.

Saturday

Daddy and Mommy
enjoy taking me to the local zoo.
My favorite animals to go see
at the zoo are the Lions and Llamas.

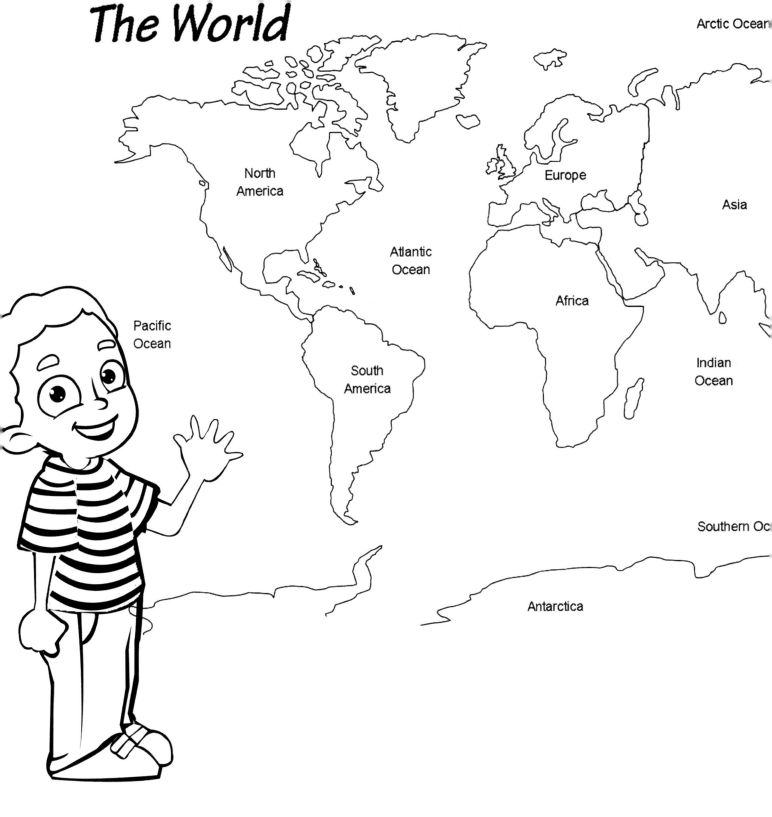

The
END

ABOUT THE AUTHOR

Kristen Mann is a professional Artists turned Author, but also Mother to her son Legend Thomas. She wanted to create a reading experience for her son that allowed him to see the image of people who were just like him on a consistent basis. After much consideration, she came up with the courage to write a children's book with her son as the lead character. Kristen hopes that children just like Legend will start to form confidence in their identity as well as learn skills such as reading comprehension. Literacy is important for her son to have and she hopes to also share the importance with the world through books like this one.

Made in the USA
Middletown, DE
20 January 2023